It's about Tim

GORING CHURCH FIRST SCHOOL
MULBERRY LANE, GORING-BY-SEA
WORTHING BN12 4RN

Day and Night

When the sun rises,
it is daytime.
When the sun sets,
it is night-time.

3

Sun

Day

Night

Earth

4

Sun

Day   Night

Earth

Most people are busy during the day, and asleep at night.

5

Measuring Time

There are 24 hours in a day and night.

People use clocks and watches to tell what time it is.

There are
60 minutes
in each hour,
and 60 seconds
in each minute.

There are
different ways
of showing and
writing the time.

7:30 A.M.

9:15 A.M.

ight o'clock

3:00 P.M.

Quarter to seven

12 o'clock

9

Days and Weeks

There are 7 days
in each week:
Monday, Tuesday,
Wednesday, Thursday,
Friday, Saturday,
and Sunday.

Our Springtime Weather Chart

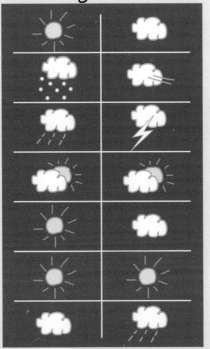

	Morning	Afternoon
Monday	sunny	cloudy
Tuesday	snowy	windy
Wednesday	rainy	stormy
Thursday	partly sunny	partly sunny
Friday	sunny	cloudy
Saturday	sunny	sunny
Sunday	cloudy	rainy

KEY

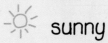 sunny

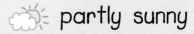 partly sunny

cloudy

windy

stormy

rainy

snowy

Monday 6

Today I told the class that my tooth fell out!

Tuesday 7

I went to gymnastics this afternoon.

Wednesday 8

We took Grandma's puppy for a walk after school.

Thursday 9

I practised my swimming for half an hour.

Friday   10

This evening, I watched a movie with my friend, Chloe.

Saturday   11

It is the weekend! I played sport then went to a party.

Sunday   12

It rained. I read books in bed and then I made biscuits.

My favourite day this week was Saturday.

People use diaries to plan and record events for each day.

Months and Years

There are about 4 weeks
in each month.
There are 12 months
in each year.
Each month has a name.

14

Days in Each Month

January 31

February 28 or 29

March 31

April 30

May 31

June 30

July 31

August 31

September 30

October 31

November 30

December 31

There are usually 365 days in a year. There is one extra day every 4 years. We call that year a leap year.

16

April

walk the dog gymnastics birthday sport movie

Sunday Monday Tuesday Wednesday Thursday Friday Saturday

People use calendars to plan and record special events in the year.

17

Seasons

Most places have
4 seasons in each year:
spring, summer, autumn,
and winter.

Seasons bring changes
in the weather.

19

Northern Hemisphere

Europe

Asia

North America

Africa

Equator

South America

Australia

Antarctica

Southern Hemisphere

20

In some countries,
people ski
in December.
In other countries,
people swim
in December.

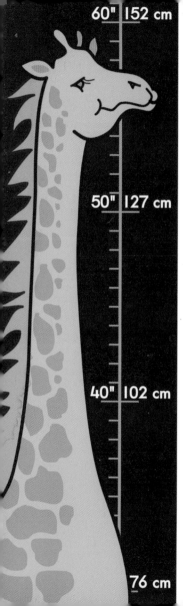

60" 152 cm

50" 127 cm

40" 102 cm

76 cm

Growing and Changing

As time goes by,
all living things change.
Some things grow and
change quickly over
a few days. Others
grow more slowly
over weeks or months.

22

Days

Weeks

Months

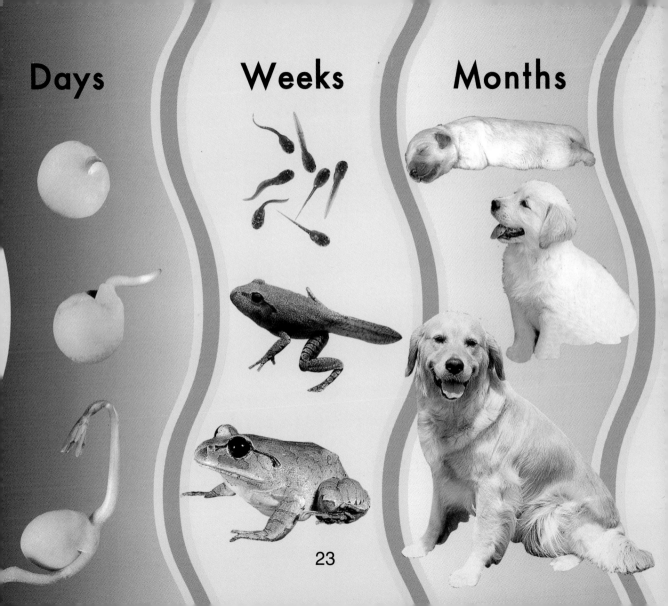

23

Index

24